Concise

Travel Guide

To

QUEENSLAND

2024-2025

Exploring the Sunshine State without

Breaking the Bank

PAUL SCOTT

|1|

WELCOME TO QUEENSLAND

Overview of Queensland

Queensland, known as the "Sunshine State," offers a diverse blend of natural wonders, modern cities, and cultural heritage. Situated in northeastern Australia, it is famous for its stunning beaches, tropical rainforests, and the world-renowned Great Barrier Reef. Queensland boasts a warm climate year-round, making it a perfect destination for travellers seeking sun, sand, and adventure.

Whether you're exploring the vibrant streets of Brisbane, enjoying the surf on the Gold Coast, or venturing into the Outback for a taste of Australia's rugged landscapes, Queensland offers a little bit of everything. Its islands, national parks, and coastal regions teem with wildlife, offering opportunities for eco-tourism and unique encounters with nature.

Key features include

The Great Barrier Reef ranks among the world's most remarkable natural wonders.

Fraser Island: The largest sand island on Earth, perfect for outdoor enthusiasts.

Daintree Rainforest: One of the oldest rainforests, home to rare plant and animal species.

Brisbane: A lively capital city filled with art, culture, and culinary experiences.

Essential Travel Tips and Safety Guidelines

Travelling in Queensland can be an unforgettable experience, but it's essential to stay prepared and informed. Here are some key tips and safety guidelines to ensure a smooth and enjoyable journey:

Weather and Climate

Queensland's tropical and subtropical climate means plenty of sunshine. Wear sunscreen (SPF 30+), sunglasses, and a hat. Heat and humidity can cause dehydration, so carry a reusable water bottle. Northern Queensland is prone to cyclones from November to April, so check weather forecasts if visiting during these months.

Health and Safety

In some areas (especially in the tropics), you'll encounter stingers (jellyfish). Swim only in designated safe zones with stinger nets. Use insect repellent to avoid bites, particularly in the evenings and in rainforest areas.

Dial 000 for police, fire, or medical emergencies.

Wildlife Awareness

Avoid swimming in rivers, estuaries, and mangroves in northern Queensland, as saltwater crocodiles inhabit these areas.

If visiting Fraser Island, keep your distance from dingoes and do not feed them. Be cautious of sharks and stingers. Always follow local guidelines for beach safety.

Driving and Road Safety

Road Rules: In Australia, vehicles drive on the left side of the road. Queensland is vast, so plan your road trips with sufficient rest stops. If driving through remote areas, carry extra water, fuel, and a first-aid kit. Inform someone of your travel route beforehand.

Cultural Etiquette and Respect

Respect Aboriginal cultural sites and ask permission before taking photos where required. Participate in cultural tours to learn more.

Queenslanders are friendly and laid-back. A warm "G'day" or "Hello" goes a long way in making connections. Smoking is banned in many public areas, including beaches and parks.

Money and Mobile Connectivity

The Australian dollar (AUD) is used. Credit cards are widely accepted, but carry cash for remote areas. Purchase a local SIM for affordable data and calls. Major networks include Telstra, Optus, and Vodafone. Download the "Emergency+" app and a weather tracking app for real-time safety alerts.

Weather Conditions and Ideal Travel Times.

Queensland's size and geography give it a varied climate, ranging from tropical rainforests in the north to subtropical and temperate regions further south. Here's a breakdown of Queensland's climate and the ideal times to visit different regions.

Summer (December to February)

Hot and humid, especially in northern Queensland. Average temperatures: 25–35°C (77–95°F). Northern areas experience heavy rainfall and thunderstorms.

Autumn (March to May)

Cooler and less humid, especially in the south. Average temperatures: 18–28°C (64–82°F). Cyclone season tapers off by April.

Winter (June to August)

Mild, dry weather with cooler nights.

Average temperatures: 10–25°C (50–77°F).

The best season for exploring the Outback and the Great Barrier Reef.

Spring (September to November)

Warm days with low humidity; ideal for outdoor activities.Average temperatures: 20–30°C (68–86°F).

Wildflower blooms in the Outback and national parks.

Regional Climate Overview

Northern Queensland (Cairns, Port Douglas, Daintree Rainforest): Tropical climate with distinct wet (Nov-Apr) and dry (May-Oct) seasons.

Best Time: May to October (dry season) for diving, snorkelling, and rainforest tours.

Central Queensland (Whitsundays, Great Barrier Reef): Warm year-round, but avoid the wet season (Dec-Apr).
Best Time: June to October for sailing and reef activities.

Southern Queensland (Brisbane, Gold Coast, Sunshine Coast): Subtropical climate with warm summers and mild winters.
Best Time: March to May or September to November for pleasant temperatures and fewer crowds.

Outback Queensland (Longreach, Winton):
Harsh desert climate with extreme heat in summer and cold in winter.
Best Time: April to September to avoid extreme heat.

Best Time for Activities

- Beach Holidays: September to November offers warm weather and ideal swimming conditions.
- Great Barrier Reef: June to October provides clear waters and fewer stingers.
- Rainforest Exploration: Visit between May and September when conditions are cooler and drier.
- Whale Watching: June to October is whale migration season along the coast.
- Outback Adventures: April to August offers comfortable temperatures for exploring.

|2|

GETTING THERE & AROUND

Major Airports and Entry Points

Queensland is well-connected to the rest of Australia and the world, with numerous airports and entry points across the state. Here's a breakdown of the key airports and transportation hubs:

International Airports

Brisbane Airport (BNE)

Queensland's largest and busiest airport, located 15 km (9 miles) from the city centre. Serves as the primary international gateway, with direct flights to Asia, the Pacific, Europe, and North America. Airtrain, taxis, rideshare, and shuttle services connect the airport to the city and beyond.

Cairns Airport (CNS)

Located in Tropical North Queensland, 7 km (4 miles) from Cairns city. Key hub for travellers heading to the Great Barrier Reef and Daintree Rainforest. Direct international flights from Asia and New Zealand, and extensive domestic connections.

Gold Coast Airport (OOL)

Straddling the Queensland-New South Wales border, 30 minutes from Surfers Paradise. International flights from New Zealand and domestic routes throughout Australia.

Domestic and Regional Airports

Sunshine Coast Airport (MCY)

Located in Marcoola, 10 km (6 miles) from Maroochydore. Domestic routes from major Australian cities like Sydney, Melbourne, and Adelaide.

Townsville Airport (TSV)

Key hub for northern Queensland, offering connections to Cairns, Brisbane, and regional centres. Gateway to Magnetic Island and the northern Outback.

Whitsunday Coast Airport (PPP)

Located near Proserpine, serving Airlie Beach and the Whitsunday Islands. Popular with travellers heading to the Great Barrier Reef and luxury resorts.

Border Crossings and Driving into Queensland

Driving from New South Wales:

- The Pacific Highway links Sydney and Brisbane, while the New England Highway offers a scenic inland route.

Cross-Border Train Services:

- NSW TrainLink and The Spirit of Queensland trains connect Brisbane with Sydney and regional towns.

Transportation Options

Getting around Queensland offers flexibility and adventure, with several transportation options to suit your itinerary and preferences. Here's a breakdown of the main ways to travel within the state:

Flights

Domestic Air Travel

Several airlines, including Qantas, Virgin Australia, Jetstar, and Rex, operate frequent flights between Queensland's cities and regional hubs.

Popular routes include Brisbane to Cairns, Brisbane to Townsville, and Cairns to the Whitsundays. Flights are the fastest way to cover long distances, especially for journeys to northern Queensland or the Outback.

Regional Airlines

Rex (Regional Express) and Alliance Airlines connect smaller towns and remote areas with major hubs. Great for accessing places like Mount Isa, Longreach, and Charleville.

Trains

The Spirit of Queensland

A long-distance train service running from Brisbane to Cairns (1,681 km/1,044 miles). Features tilt-train technology, offering a comfortable and scenic way to explore the coast. Sleeper cabins, dining options, and Wi-Fi are available for long journeys.

The Spirit of the Outback

Travels from Brisbane to Longreach, offering a glimpse into Queensland's rural heartland.

A great option for travellers interested in Outback culture, history, and landscapes.

The Gulflander and Savannahlander

Unique heritage rail services in northern Queensland, known for scenic routes and slow-paced travel through the wilderness.

Ideal for travellers seeking an authentic, off-the-beaten-track experience.

|3|

ROAD TRIPS AND DRIVING

Highways and Roads

Queensland boasts well-maintained highways like the Bruce Highway (linking Brisbane to Cairns) and the Pacific Highway (connecting Brisbane to New South Wales). Inland routes like the Warrego Highway provide access to Outback towns and the Darling Downs.

Campervans and Rentals

Renting a car or campervan is popular for exploring Queensland's diverse landscapes.

Campervan parks are common along the coast and in national parks, allowing for budget-friendly, scenic stays.

Iconic Road Trips

Great Barrier Reef Drive: Cairns to Cape Tribulation along the scenic coast.

Savannah Way: An epic cross-country drive from Cairns to the Northern Territory.

Pacific Coast Way: Brisbane to Cairns, with stops at beaches, rainforests, and the Whitsundays.

Public Buses and Coaches

Greyhound Australia

Operates long-distance buses connecting Brisbane, Cairns, the Gold Coast, and regional towns.

Offers hop-on-hop-off passes for flexible travel. Major cities like Brisbane, Gold Coast, and Sunshine Coast have reliable public buses and tram services. TransLink manages buses, trains, and ferries across South East Queensland.

Queensland Museum

Located at South Bank, the Queensland Museum offers insights into the natural history, cultural heritage, and scientific achievements of Queensland and Australia. Highlights include exhibits on Dinosaurs, Wildlife, and Cultural Heritage, along with rotating exhibitions that explore various themes.

Sciencentre:

An interactive area that engages visitors with hands-on science experiences, perfect for families and curious minds.

Museum of Brisbane

Located in the iconic Brisbane City Hall, the Museum of Brisbane celebrates the city's history and cultural heritage. Focuses on Brisbane's past, present, and future through engaging exhibitions that cover topics like architecture, community, and significant historical events.

Institute of Modern Art (IMA)

A leading contemporary art space located in the heart of Brisbane, the IMA supports innovative and experimental art practices.

Features a dynamic program of contemporary exhibitions, artist talks, and workshops, showcasing emerging and established artists from Australia and beyond.

Top Cafés and Nightlife Spots

Brisbane's café culture and nightlife scene are vibrant and diverse, reflecting the city's laid-back yet cosmopolitan vibe. Here's a guide to some of the top cafés and nightlife spots to check out during your visit:

Campo Espresso

Location at South Brisbane

Renowned for its quality coffee and a selection of house-made pastries, Campo Espresso is a favourite among locals. The cosy atmosphere makes it perfect for a relaxed coffee break.

Pawpaw Café

Location at South Brisbane

This popular café is known for its fresh, vibrant dishes with Asian influences. Its lush garden setting and excellent brunch menu make it a must-visit spot.

The Gunshop Café

Location at West End

A Brisbane institution, The Gunshop Café offers a seasonal menu and great coffee in a charming, rustic setting. Their breakfast and brunch options are particularly popular.

Coffee Anthology

Location at Fortitude Valley

A specialty coffee shop that focuses on high-quality beans sourced from around the world. They offer a variety of brewing methods and a rotating selection of single-origin coffees.

Dandelion & Driftwood

Location at Grange

A beautifully designed café with an emphasis on sustainability and ethical sourcing. Dandelion & Driftwood serves delicious coffee and light bites in a serene environment.

Top Nightlife Spots

Fortitude Valley

Brisbane's nightlife hub, known for its vibrant atmosphere and variety of bars and clubs. Popular venues include Cloudland, a stunning multi-level bar, and The Brightside, known for live music and events.

Howard Smith Wharves

A riverside destination with a range of bars and restaurants. Felons Brewing Co. offers craft beers with stunning views of the Story Bridge, while Mr. Percival's is a lively bar with a relaxed vibe.

The Lyric Theatre

Located at Brisbane's South Bank

Home to a variety of live performances, including theatre, concerts, and dance shows. A great spot to enjoy a cultural night out.

The Valley Drive-In

Location at Fortitude Valley

A unique experience that combines a bar, a drive-in cinema, and a retro vibe. Enjoy classic films while sipping on cocktails and munching on popcorn.

The Gresham

Located at Brisbane CBD

A stylish bar known for its extensive whiskey selection and classic cocktails. The Gresham combines an elegant atmosphere with a relaxed vibe, making it ideal for a night out.

|4|

THE GOLD COAST

Best Beaches (Surfers Paradise, Burleigh Heads)

The Gold Coast is renowned for its stunning coastline, vibrant beach culture, and world-class surf. Here are two of the best beaches to visit when exploring this iconic destination:

Surfers Paradise

Surfers Paradise is arguably the most famous beach on the Gold Coast, known for its golden sands, high-rise skyline, and bustling atmosphere. It's a hotspot for both tourists and locals, offering a wide range of activities and amenities. The beach is perfect for surfers of all levels, with consistent waves and surf schools available for beginners.

Explore the nightly markets along the beachfront, where you can find local crafts, art, and delicious street food. Surfers Paradise is known for its vibrant nightlife, with a variety of bars, clubs, and restaurants lining the streets. The beach is well-equipped with amenities such as showers, restrooms, lifeguards, and beachfront dining options.

Burleigh Heads

Burleigh Heads is a more laid-back beach compared to Surfers Paradise, famous for its natural beauty and relaxed atmosphere. Surrounded by lush national parkland, it offers stunning views and a family-friendly vibe.

Known for its excellent surf breaks, Burleigh is popular among experienced surfers and swimmers. The beach is patrolled by lifeguards, ensuring safety for families.

Enjoy scenic walking trails that lead to breathtaking lookout points with views of the coastline. The park is home to diverse wildlife and ancient volcanic rock formations. There are plenty of grassy areas and picnic spots perfect for a relaxed day by the beach. Public BBQ facilities are also available. Burleigh Heads boasts a variety of trendy cafés and restaurants, with options ranging from casual beachside dining to upscale eateries. The vibrant café scene is perfect for enjoying breakfast or lunch with ocean views.

Thrilling Theme Parks

The Gold Coast is home to some of the most exciting theme parks in Australia, offering a wide range of attractions that cater to thrill-seekers, families, and everyone in between. Here's a guide to the top theme parks you can't miss:

Dreamworld

As Australia's largest theme park, Dreamworld offers an array of thrilling rides, animal experiences, and family-friendly attractions.

Thrilling Rides:

Tower of Terror X: A high-speed roller coaster that launches riders from 0 to 100 km/h in just a few seconds, providing breathtaking views of the Gold Coast.

The Claw: A giant pendulum ride that swings riders high into the air for an adrenaline-pumping experience.

Wildlife Experiences:

Dreamworld is home to Dreamworld Wildlife Foundation, where visitors can encounter Australian animals, including koalas, kangaroos, and crocodiles.

Warner Bros. Movie World

This Hollywood-themed park brings the magic of movies to life with exhilarating rides, live shows, and immersive experiences.

Thrilling Rides:

DC Rivals HyperCoaster: One of the tallest and longest coasters in the Southern Hemisphere, featuring multiple inversions and a stunning drop.
Justice League 3D – The Ride: An interactive dark ride where guests join Batman and other DC heroes to save the day using laser blasters.
Live stunt shows and character meet-and-greets offer a chance to see beloved movie characters and witness incredible performances.

Paradise Country

A unique experience that showcases Australian farm life, with opportunities to interact with animals and enjoy live shows.

While not as thrill-focused as other parks, Paradise Country offers family-friendly activities like animal feeding, sheep shearing demonstrations, and tractor rides.

Experience Australian culture through traditional performances, including whip cracking and sheep dog demonstrations.

|5|

THE GREAT BARRIER REEF

Best Islands to Visit

The Great Barrier Reef is one of the world's most breathtaking natural wonders, featuring stunning islands with diverse ecosystems, crystal-clear waters, and vibrant marine life. Here are some of the best islands to explore when visiting the Great Barrier Reef:

Hamilton Island

Hamilton Island is the largest inhabited island in the Whitsundays and offers a range of luxurious accommodations, dining options, and activities. Explore the underwater world at nearby reefs, including the famous Great Barrier Reef Marine Park. Enjoy swimming, sunbathing, and various water sports at this beautiful beach.

Play a round at the championship golf course with stunning views of the surrounding islands.

Accessible by direct flights from major cities like Brisbane and Sydney, as well as ferry services from the mainland.

Whitsunday Islands

A group of 74 islands known for their stunning beaches and lush rainforests. Whitehaven Beach, often regarded as one of the best beaches in the world, is located here.

Famous for its pure silica sand and turquoise waters, it's perfect for swimming, picnicking, and relaxing. Explore the vibrant marine life and coral reefs surrounding the islands. Various sailing tours and charters are available. A short hike offers panoramic views of the stunning swirling sands and the surrounding waters.

Lizard Island

A remote island known for its exclusivity, Lizard Island is a luxury getaway with beautiful beaches and pristine coral reefs.

World-class diving opportunities with access to the nearby Cod Hole and Osprey Reef, known for encounters with large marine life like potato cod and reef sharks. Explore the island's walking trails, leading to scenic lookouts and diverse wildlife.

Fitzroy Island

A tropical paradise located just 45 minutes by ferry from Cairns, Fitzroy Island offers a mix of adventure and relaxation.

The island has an excellent snorkelling area right off the beach, with coral reefs and colourful fish easily accessible. Explore walking trails leading to the summit of the island for stunning views of the reef and surrounding waters. Enjoy kayaking, paddleboarding, and relaxing on the beautiful beaches.

Heron Island

Located on the southern Great Barrier Reef, Heron Island is a coral cay famous for its snorkelling and diving opportunities. With direct access to the reef, it's perfect for underwater exploration, featuring diverse marine life and vibrant coral gardens.

Depending on the season (November to February), visitors can witness green sea turtles nesting on the island. Guided walks provide insights into the island's ecosystems and the marine environment.

Green Island

A small coral cay located just 27 kilometres from Cairns, Green Island is a popular day trip destination. Accessible coral reefs make it easy for visitors to snorkel directly from the beach. A great option for those who prefer to stay dry while exploring the underwater world. Short walking trails take you through the island's lush rainforest, showcasing its unique flora and fauna.

Snorkeling and Diving Sites

The Great Barrier Reef is renowned for its stunning underwater landscapes, diverse marine life, and vibrant coral formations. Here are some of the best snorkelling and diving sites to explore when visiting this UNESCO World Heritage site.

Cod Hole

Located Near Lizard Island

Cod Hole is famous for its large potato cod that swim freely with divers, providing a unique experience. Encounter friendly potato cod, colourful reef fish, and various species of coral. Suitable for all levels, with depths ranging from 10 to 30 metres.

Agincourt Reef

Located at the Outer Barrier Reef, near Port Douglas. Agincourt Reef features breathtaking coral formations and vibrant marine ecosystems, with several dive sites available.

Spot turtles, reef sharks, and a plethora of tropical fish among stunning coral gardens.

Offers diverse diving options, including shallow coral gardens for snorkelers and deeper sites for experienced divers.

Osprey Reef

Located at Far North Queensland, part of the Coral Sea. A remote dive site renowned for its dramatic underwater landscapes and rich biodiversity.

Experience encounters with large pelagic species, including sharks, rays, and schools of fish.

Best suited for experienced divers, with depths exceeding 30 metres. Features thrilling wall dives and stunning drop-offs.

Great Barrier Island

Located Near Cairns

A picturesque spot known for its vibrant coral reefs and diverse marine life, perfect for both snorkelling and diving. Common sightings include clownfish, angelfish, and large schools of butterflyfish, along with soft corals. Accessible to divers of all levels, with shallow areas for snorkelers and deeper sections for advanced divers.

The Ribbon Reefs

Located North of Port Douglas

A series of beautiful, elongated reefs known for their stunning coral formations and excellent visibility. Rich in biodiversity, with opportunities to see turtles, nudibranchs, and large schools of fish.

Offers a variety of dive sites, catering to both snorkelers and advanced divers, with depths ranging from shallow to deeper dives.

|6|

CAIRNS AND TROPICAL NORTH QUEENSLAND

Rainforest Adventures (Daintree, Kuranda)

Tropical North Queensland is a paradise for nature lovers, boasting lush rainforests, diverse ecosystems, and stunning landscapes. Two of the most popular rainforest destinations in this region are Daintree Rainforest and Kuranda. Here's a guide to exploring the incredible rainforest adventures available in these areas:

Daintree Rainforest

The Daintree Rainforest is one of the oldest rainforests in the world, recognized for its incredible biodiversity and stunning scenery. It's part of the larger Daintree National Park, a UNESCO World Heritage site.

Join a guided tour to learn about the rainforest's unique flora and fauna. Many tours offer the chance to spot wildlife like cassowaries, crocodiles, and various bird species. Explore the Daintree River on a guided cruise to see crocodiles in their natural habitat and learn about the ecosystem.

There are several walking trails to explore, such as the Mossman Gorge and Jindalba Boardwalk, where visitors can immerse themselves in the lush surroundings. Visit this unique location where the rainforest meets the reef, offering stunning beaches and hiking opportunities.

Kuranda

Kuranda is a charming village located in the rainforest, known for its stunning scenery, vibrant markets, and cultural experiences. Accessible by scenic railway or skyrail, it's a popular day trip from Cairns.

Experience breathtaking views as you glide above the rainforest canopy on the Skyrail. Stop at mid-stations to explore walking trails and learn about the rainforest's ecology.

Enjoy a scenic train ride through the mountains, passing waterfalls and lush landscapes while learning about the history of the area. Explore the local markets featuring handmade crafts, Aboriginal art, and delicious food. It's a great place to find unique souvenirs. Experience Australia's wildlife up close with koalas, kangaroos, and more. Enjoy an amphibious army duck tour through the rainforest and learn about traditional Aboriginal culture.

Exploring Cairns and the Esplanade Lagoon

Cairns, the gateway to the Great Barrier Reef, is a vibrant city in Tropical North Queensland known for its stunning natural beauty, outdoor activities, and relaxed atmosphere. One of the highlights of Cairns is the Esplanade Lagoon, a picturesque waterfront area that offers a variety of recreational opportunities and stunning views. Here's a guide to exploring Cairns and the Esplanade Lagoon:

Cairns Esplanade

The Cairns Esplanade stretches along the waterfront and is a hub for outdoor activities, dining, and relaxation. It features beautiful parklands, walking and cycling paths, and stunning views of Trinity Inlet and the surrounding mountains. Enjoy a leisurely stroll or bike ride along the Esplanade, with dedicated pathways offering scenic views of the water and surrounding landscapes.

The grassy areas and picnic spots along the Esplanade are perfect for enjoying a meal with family and friends. Picnic tables and BBQ facilities are available. Families can take advantage of the children's playground, featuring climbing structures and water play areas, making it a great spot for kids to have fun.

Esplanade Lagoon

The Esplanade Lagoon is a large, man-made swimming lagoon that offers a safe and family-friendly alternative to swimming in the ocean. It features sandy beaches, shallow areas for children, and deeper sections for adults.

The lagoon is open to the public and free to use, making it a popular destination for both locals and tourists. The lagoon is monitored by lifeguards, ensuring a safe swimming environment for visitors.

Facilities include showers, restrooms, and shaded areas, making it comfortable for visitors to spend the day.

Enjoy a refreshing swim in the lagoon while taking in the beautiful views of the surrounding landscape. Relax on the sandy beach areas or on the grassy banks, perfect for sunbathing or reading a book. The lagoon area often hosts community events, markets, and outdoor movie nights, providing entertainment throughout the year.

Nearby Attractions

Cairns Botanic Gardens

Just a short distance from the Esplanade, these gardens showcase tropical plants and offer walking trails, picnic spots, and a café.

Take a day trip to Kuranda to experience the scenic railway and skyrail, offering breathtaking views of the rainforest and surrounding mountains.

Cairns is the main departure point for various reef tours, offering opportunities for snorkelling, diving, and exploring the iconic Great Barrier Reef.

|7|

OUTBACK QUEENSLAND

Outback Queensland is a vast and captivating region known for its unique landscapes, rich history, and vibrant culture. Two of its prominent towns, Charleville and Longreach, offer visitors a glimpse into the heritage of Australia's outback, showcasing its pioneering spirit and historical significance. Here's a guide to exploring the history and heritage of Charleville and Longreach.

Charleville

Charleville is the largest town in the Mulga Lands region and serves as a gateway to the Outback. Known for its friendly atmosphere and historical significance, Charleville has a rich Indigenous and European heritage.

Visit the base of this iconic Australian medical service, established in 1928. The museum offers informative displays about the service's history and its role in providing healthcare to remote areas.

This beautifully restored 19th-century home offers a glimpse into the town's early days. Guided tours reveal stories of the families who lived there and the history of the region. Learn about the stars and planets in the Southern Hemisphere through interactive exhibits. The centre also offers stargazing experiences, providing a unique perspective on the outback's clear night skies.

Longreach

Longreach is renowned as the birthplace of Australia's national airline and is a vital hub for the cattle industry. The town is steeped in history, offering a variety of attractions that celebrate its heritage.

This iconic museum showcases the history of Australia's pastoralists and the significant role they played in the development of the Outback. The exhibits include artefacts, photographs, and live demonstrations of working dogs and cattle.

Discover the story of Qantas, one of the world's oldest airlines, at this museum. It features interactive displays, historical aircraft, and guided tours, including a walk through the iconic Boeing 747. Housed in a historic power station, this museum showcases the region's technological history, including exhibits on telecommunications, transport, and early electricity generation.

Events and Festivals

Charleville Camel Races

An annual event that draws visitors from across the country, this quirky race features camels competing in a fun and festive atmosphere, showcasing the unique culture of the outback.

Longreach's Outback Festival

Held every two years, this festival celebrates the region's history with a variety of events, including a street parade, live music, and traditional bush activities.

Practical Tips for Visiting

Charleville and Longreach are accessible by road and air, with regional flights connecting them to larger cities like Brisbane. Consider renting a 4WD vehicle for a true outback experience.

Both towns offer a range of accommodations, from motels and hotels to camping options, allowing visitors to choose based on their preferences and budget. The cooler months (April to September) are ideal for visiting, as temperatures are more comfortable for outdoor activities.

Dinosaur Trails

Outback Queensland is renowned for its rich prehistoric history, offering visitors the chance to explore Dinosaur Trails that showcase significant fossil sites and ancient landscapes. These trails provide an exciting opportunity to learn about Australia's dinosaur heritage, see fossil remains, and experience the beautiful scenery of the Outback. Here's a guide to exploring the Dinosaur Trails in Outback Queensland.

What is the Dinosaur Trail?

The Dinosaur Trail is a designated route that stretches through Outback Queensland, connecting several key towns and sites significant for dinosaur fossils and exhibitions. The trail allows visitors to discover the fascinating history of Australia's prehistoric giants while enjoying the rugged beauty of the Outback.

Key Locations Along the Dinosaur Trail

Winton

Winton is known as the "Dinosaur Capital of Australia" and is home to some of the most important fossil finds.

This museum is a must-visit for dinosaur enthusiasts. It features extensive exhibits on dinosaur fossils, including life-size skeletons and interactive displays. The museum also offers guided tours to its fossil preparation lab, where visitors can watch palaeontologists at work. Visit the site of the world's only known dinosaur stampede, where fossilised footprints of small dinosaurs can be seen. The interpretative centre provides insights into the events that took place millions of years ago.

Richmond

Richmond is famous for its marine fossils and is home to significant dinosaur discoveries.

The centre showcases an impressive collection of fossils, including the skeleton of a Megalania (a giant lizard) and ancient marine reptiles. Guided tours and workshops are available for those interested in fossil hunting. Richmond offers numerous opportunities for fossil hunting along designated trails and sites, where visitors can discover remnants of ancient creatures.

Hughenden

Known for its dinosaur finds, Hughenden provides insights into Australia's prehistoric past.

This museum features a range of dinosaur exhibits, including life-sized replicas and fossils. The museum highlights the region's paleontological significance and offers interactive displays for visitors.

|8|

THE WHITSUNDAYS

The Whitsundays, a stunning group of 74 islands off the coast of Queensland, are renowned for their pristine beaches, crystal-clear waters, and vibrant marine life. This tropical paradise offers a perfect blend of adventure and relaxation, making it a sought-after destination for sailing enthusiasts and luxury travellers. Here's a guide to exploring the sailing adventures and luxury resorts of the Whitsundays.

Sailing Adventures

The Whitsundays are famous for their sailing opportunities, with favourable winds and picturesque scenery making it a sailor's paradise. Whether you're an experienced sailor or a beginner, there are plenty of options to explore these beautiful islands.

Types of Sailing Tours

Day Cruises

Various operators offer full-day sailing tours that include visits to iconic sites, snorkelling, and meals onboard. These cruises provide a fantastic way to experience the beauty of the Whitsundays in a short time. For those looking for a more independent experience, bareboat charters allow you to sail at your own pace. Choose from a range of vessels, from small yachts to larger catamarans, and explore hidden coves and secluded beaches.

Indulge in a luxury sailing experience with private charters that provide personalised service, gourmet meals, and exclusive access to stunning locations. Enjoy sailing with a small group or charter a yacht for a romantic getaway.

Luxury Resorts

The Whitsundays are home to some of Australia's most luxurious resorts, offering world-class amenities, stunning views, and unparalleled service. These resorts provide the perfect base for exploring the islands while enjoying a relaxing getaway.

- Hamilton Island Resort:
As one of the largest resorts in the Whitsundays, Hamilton Island offers a range of accommodations, from luxury hotels to private villas. Enjoy a variety of dining options, pools, and direct access to sailing and water activities.

- Qualia Resort:
Located on Hamilton Island, Qualia is an exclusive luxury resort known for its stunning views, private beaches, and exceptional service. Guests can indulge in spa treatments, fine dining, and unique experiences like guided sailing trips.

- Hayman Island Resort:

This iconic resort is situated on Hayman Island and offers luxury accommodations with beautiful views of the Coral Sea. Guests can enjoy a range of activities, including water sports, fine dining, and relaxing at the spa.

Eco-Tourism and Local Wildlife

The Whitsundays are committed to eco-tourism, focusing on sustainability and preserving the natural beauty of the islands and the surrounding Great Barrier Reef. Visitors can engage in eco-friendly activities while experiencing the diverse wildlife of the region. Participate in guided tours that educate visitors about the unique ecosystems of the Whitsundays, including rainforest walks and wildlife spotting.

Some operators offer eco-tours that include marine conservation activities, such as reef restoration projects and educational experiences about marine life. Keep an eye out for native wildlife, including kangaroos, wallabies, and a variety of bird species on the islands. Dolphins and whales can also be spotted in the surrounding waters, particularly during migration seasons.

|9|

FRASER ISLAND

Fraser Island, recognized as the world's largest sand island, is a UNESCO World Heritage site located off the southeastern coast of Queensland. Renowned for its stunning landscapes, pristine beaches, and unique ecosystems, it offers visitors an unforgettable adventure. Here's a guide to exploring Fraser Island, including 4WD adventures, picturesque lakes, and incredible wildlife encounters.

4WD Adventures and Camping Spots

Fraser Island is best explored by 4WD vehicles due to its sandy terrain and diverse landscapes. The island offers a range of off-road trails that lead to breathtaking natural attractions, making it a haven for adventure enthusiasts.

4WD Adventures

Beach Driving

The eastern beach of Fraser Island serves as a highway, allowing visitors to drive along the coastline. You'll encounter stunning views, the iconic Maheno Shipwreck, and plenty of opportunities for beach fishing and picnicking.

Explore inland tracks that take you through lush rainforests, towering eucalyptus trees, and ancient sand dunes. Key spots to visit include Central Station and the Wanggoolba Creek.

Camping Spots

Fraser Island offers several designated camping areas, such as Cathedrals on Fraser, Dilli Village, and Happy Valley. These spots provide amenities and proximity to various attractions, making them ideal for nature lovers.

Camping on Fraser Island requires a permit, which can be obtained online or at the Visitor Information Centre. Be prepared with adequate supplies, including water, food, and camping gear, as facilities can be limited.

Lake McKenzie and Eli Creek

Lake McKenzie and Eli Creek are two of Fraser Island's most popular natural attractions, offering stunning beauty and opportunities for relaxation and recreation.

Lake McKenzie

Lake McKenzie is a stunning perched lake with crystal-clear waters and soft white sandy shores. Its unique ecosystem is home to diverse flora and fauna, making it a serene spot for swimming and sunbathing. The sandy bottom is soft, making it an ideal spot for relaxing in the sun. Facilities at Lake McKenzie include picnic tables and toilets, making it a great spot for a leisurely lunch amidst the beautiful scenery.

Eli Creek

Eli Creek is one of the largest freshwater creeks on Fraser Island, known for its gentle flow and picturesque surroundings. It's an excellent spot for families and those looking to cool off. Visitors can enjoy swimming in the clear waters or floating along the creek's gentle current. A boardwalk leads to the creek, providing an easy walk through the rainforest and offering opportunities for birdwatching and photography.

Fraser Island is home to diverse wildlife, making it an exciting destination for nature lovers. From the iconic dingoes to a variety of bird species, wildlife encounters are a highlight of any visit. Fraser Island is known for its population of purebred dingoes, which are often spotted along the beaches and in the forests. While they are fascinating to observe, visitors are advised to maintain a safe distance and not to feed them.

Practical Tips for Visiting Fraser Island

The ideal time to visit Fraser Island is during the dry season (April to October), when the weather is cooler, and the roads are more accessible.

Access to Fraser Island is via ferry from Hervey Bay or Rainbow Beach. Make sure to book your ferry in advance, especially during peak season. Essential items to pack include food and water, a first aid kit, insect repellent, sunscreen, and a camera to capture the breathtaking landscapes.

|10|

QUEENSLAND'S FOOD AND WINE SCENE

Queensland is renowned for its diverse and vibrant food and wine scene, influenced by its unique geography, climate, and cultural heritage. From fresh seafood and tropical fruits to world-class wines, the state offers a culinary experience that reflects its rich agricultural resources. Here's a guide to exploring Queensland's food and wine culture, including regional specialties, wine regions, and exciting food festivals.

Regional Specialties and Iconic Dishes

Queensland's culinary landscape is shaped by its coastal location, fertile lands, and multicultural influences. Here are some regional specialties and iconic dishes you must try while visiting.

Seafood

Moreton Bay Bugs: These sweet and tender shellfish are a local delicacy, often served grilled or in salads.

Mud Crabs: Caught fresh from Queensland's waters, mud crabs are a popular choice for seafood lovers. They can be enjoyed steamed, in curries, or simply with garlic butter.

Tropical Fruits:

Pineapples: The Sunshine Coast is known for its juicy pineapples, often used in salads, desserts, and tropical drinks.

Mangoes: Queensland produces some of the best mangoes in Australia, particularly in the Northern regions. Enjoy them fresh, in smoothies, or as a chutney.

Local Dishes

Barramundi: This iconic fish is often grilled, pan-fried, or served in fish tacos, showcasing Queensland's rich seafood heritage.

Anzac Biscuits: Originating during World War I, these sweet biscuits made with oats and coconut are a nostalgic treat found in many cafes across the state.

Wine Regions (Granite Belt and Beyond)

Queensland is home to several wine regions that produce a diverse range of wines, particularly known for their innovative blends and cool-climate varieties.

Granite Belt

Located near the border of New South Wales, the Granite Belt is Queensland's premier wine region, known for its granite soils and high altitude, which create ideal conditions for grape growing.

Wines

The region is famous for its Shiraz, Chardonnay, and Cabernet Sauvignon. Many wineries also produce exceptional alternative varieties like Verdelho and Tempranillo.

- Wineries to Visit:

Ballandean Estate Wines: Known for its extensive range of wines, this family-owned winery offers tastings and a beautiful vineyard setting.

Sutton's Juice Factory: A unique winery that specialises in fruit wines and juices, providing a different tasting experience.

- South Burnett: This emerging wine region is gaining recognition for its quality wines, particularly Chardonnay and Cabernet Sauvignon.

- Sunshine Coast Hinterland: Known for boutique wineries and stunning views, this area produces a variety of wines, including Shiraz and Sparkling.

Food Festivals and Farmers Markets

Queensland hosts a range of food festivals and farmers markets that celebrate local produce, culinary talent, and the vibrant food culture of the state.

Food Festivals

- Noosa Food and Wine Festival: Held annually, this festival showcases local chefs, wineries, and producers. Attendees can enjoy gourmet food tastings, cooking demonstrations, and wine pairings.

- Brisbane Gourmet Food and Wine Festival: A celebration of local and international cuisine, this festival features food stalls, wine tastings, and celebrity chef appearances.

- Tropical North Queensland Food Festival: This event celebrates the rich agricultural bounty of the region, featuring local produce, cooking workshops, and tastings.

Farmers Markets

- Brisbane City Market: Held every Wednesday and Saturday, this market features fresh produce, artisanal foods, and handmade goods from local farmers and vendors.

- Eumundi Markets: Located near Noosa, these markets are famous for their fresh produce, handmade crafts, and delicious street food. They attract both locals and tourists alike.

- Cairns Esplanade Markets: Held every Saturday, this market offers a variety of fresh produce, crafts, and local delicacies, providing a taste of the tropical lifestyle.

|11|

ADVENTURE AND OUTDOOR ACTIVITIES

Queensland is a playground for adventure enthusiasts, offering a diverse range of outdoor activities that cater to thrill-seekers and nature lovers alike. From skydiving over stunning landscapes to hiking through lush rainforests, the state boasts endless opportunities for adventure. Here's a guide to some of the best activities to experience during your visit.

Skydiving

Experience the ultimate adrenaline rush by skydiving over Queensland's breathtaking scenery. With stunning views of the coastline, Great Barrier Reef, and hinterlands, this is a must-do for thrill-seekers.

Popular Locations

- Cairns: Dive over the beautiful Great Barrier Reef and witness the vibrant colours of the coral below.

- Gold Coast: Jump over the pristine beaches and lush hinterlands for a truly unforgettable experience.

Hot Air Ballooning

For a more serene adventure, hot air ballooning offers a peaceful way to take in Queensland's landscapes. Drift high above the ground as the sun rises and enjoy panoramic views of the countryside.

- Atherton Tablelands: Known for its stunning scenery and lush landscapes, this area is a popular spot for hot air balloon rides.

- Brisbane Valley: Experience breathtaking views of rolling hills and vineyards as you glide through the sky.

Bungy Jumping

Experience the thrill of bungy jumping from a height of 50 metres at the AJ Hackett Bungy in Cairns. With the stunning rainforest as your backdrop, this is an exhilarating way to challenge your limits.

Hiking Trails

Queensland is home to a variety of hiking trails and scenic walks that showcase the region's natural beauty, from ancient rainforests to stunning coastal views.

Popular Hiking Trails

 - Lamington National Park:

   - Trail: Box Forest Circuit (10.5 km)

This circuit takes you through lush rainforest, past waterfalls, and offers stunning views of the surrounding landscape.

- Daintree National Park
  - Trail: Mossman Gorge Circuit (2 km)

A short but rewarding hike through one of the oldest rainforests in the world, featuring beautiful scenery and swimming spots in the river.

- Glass House Mountains:
  - Trail: Mount Ngungun Summit Track (2.8 km)

This hike leads to the summit of Mount Ngungun, offering panoramic views of the Glass House Mountains and the surrounding countryside.

Scenic Walks:
- Queensland Coastal Walk:
  - Overview: A series of trails that run along Queensland's coastline, offering stunning ocean views and access to beautiful beaches.
- Brisbane Riverwalk:
  - Overview: A picturesque walking path along the Brisbane River, perfect for leisurely strolls, jogging, or cycling while enjoying the city skyline.

FAMILY-FRIENDLY ACTIVITIES AND DESTINATIONS

Queensland is an ideal destination for families, offering a wide variety of activities and attractions that cater to children of all ages. From interactive museums to wildlife experiences, the state is packed with fun and educational opportunities. Here's a guide to some of the best family-friendly activities and destinations in Queensland.

Australia Zoo

Located on the Sunshine Coast, Australia Zoo is one of the most famous wildlife parks in Australia, founded by the late Steve Irwin. It offers an immersive experience with a wide variety of animals.

Watch thrilling crocodile feeding demonstrations and learn about wildlife conservation.

Koala Encounters: Get up close and personal with koalas and kangaroos, with opportunities for photos.

Sea Life Sunshine Coast Aquarium

This aquarium features marine life from local waters and around the globe, offering interactive exhibits and educational experiences.

Underwater Tunnel: Walk through the underwater tunnel and see sharks, rays, and colourful fish swimming above you. Enjoy live shows featuring trained seals that entertain while educating visitors about marine conservation.

Lone Pine Koala Sanctuary

Located in Brisbane, Lone Pine is the world's first and largest koala sanctuary, home to over 130 koalas and many other Australian animals. Children can hold and take photos with a koala (additional fee applies). Watch fascinating flying displays from hawks, eagles, and owls in a live show.

Kids-Friendly Beaches and Playgrounds

Surfers Paradise Beach

Famous for its golden sands and family-friendly atmosphere, Surfers Paradise Beach is perfect for a day of sun, sand, and surf.

Enjoy peace of mind knowing the beach is patrolled by lifeguards, ensuring safety for families. Rent equipment for paddleboarding or try a family-friendly surfing lesson.

Noosa Main Beach

A sheltered beach with calm waters, Noosa Main Beach is perfect for families with young children. Located near the beach, the playground offers a safe space for kids to play while parents relax nearby. Enjoy a family picnic with nearby cafes and restaurants for added convenience.

|13|

FESTIVALS AND EVENTS

Queensland is vibrant with a diverse range of festivals and events throughout the year, showcasing the state's rich culture, artistic talents, and outdoor lifestyle. From local celebrations to large-scale festivals, there's something for everyone to enjoy. Here's a guide to some of the most exciting festivals and events in Queensland.

Cultural Festivals and Local Celebrations
Brisbane Festival

Held annually in September, the Brisbane Festival is a month-long celebration of arts and culture, featuring a variety of performances, installations, and events. A spectacular fireworks display over the Brisbane River, marking the festival's grand finale. Showcases local and international artists, including theatre, dance, and circus acts.

Woodford Folk Festival:

This iconic festival takes place in Woodford, just north of Brisbane, over six days during the New Year period, celebrating music, arts, and culture.

Live Music: Featuring over 200 performances across various stages, showcasing folk, world, and contemporary music. Participate in diverse workshops ranging from arts and crafts to yoga and sustainable living.

Cairns Indigenous Art Fair

Celebrating Indigenous culture and arts, this fair occurs annually in July and showcases works from Indigenous artists across Queensland.

Discover traditional and contemporary Indigenous art, including paintings, sculpture, and textiles.

Enjoy live performances, storytelling, and workshops led by Indigenous artists.

Big Sound Festival (Brisbane)

A premier music industry festival held annually in September, Big Sound showcases emerging Australian artists and offers networking opportunities for industry professionals.

Discover new talent across various venues in Brisbane's Fortitude Valley. Engage with industry leaders and artists through informative sessions.

Noosa Food and Wine Festival

This festival, held in May, celebrates Queensland's culinary scene with tastings, cooking demonstrations, and events featuring local and international chefs.

Participate in hands-on cooking classes with renowned chefs. Enjoy tastings from local wineries and producers, paired with gourmet dishes.

Sports and Adventure Events

Gold Coast Marathon

Taking place annually in July, the Gold Coast Marathon is a premier running event that attracts thousands of participants from around the world.

Offers various races, including a marathon, half-marathon, 10km, and a fun run for families. Runners enjoy beautiful coastal views along the Gold Coast, making it a popular event for both serious athletes and casual participants.

Noosa Triathlon

One of the largest triathlons in the Southern Hemisphere, held annually in November, attracting elite athletes and novices alike.

A family-friendly event with live entertainment, food stalls, and activities for spectators. Offers different distances and categories, making it accessible for all ages and fitness levels.

|14|

ACCOMMODATION OPTIONS

Queensland offers a diverse range of accommodation options to suit every traveller's needs and budget, from luxurious resorts to budget-friendly hostels. Whether you're looking for a lavish getaway, a cosy retreat, or a unique experience, Queensland has something for everyone. Here's a guide to the various accommodation options available throughout the state.

Luxury Resorts and Boutique Hotels
InterContinental Sanctuary Cove Resort

This stunning resort features a blend of luxury and tranquillity, set on the Gold Coast's scenic waterways. Multiple swimming pools, a spa, fine dining options, and a golf course. The resort's charming architecture and lush gardens create a peaceful oasis for relaxation.

Qualia Resort

A luxurious retreat on Hamilton Island, Qualia is known for its stunning views of the Great Barrier Reef and high-end amenities.

YHA Brisbane City

A centrally located hostel that offers affordable accommodation for backpackers and budget travelers.A mix of dormitory-style accommodations and private rooms to suit various preferences.

A communal kitchen, lounge, and outdoor terrace for socialising with other travellers.

Nomads Brisbane

A lively hostel known for its friendly atmosphere and great location in the heart of Brisbane.

Regular events and outings organised for guests, making it easy to meet fellow travellers.

On-site bar and café, plus a travel desk for booking tours and activities.

Eco-Friendly Lodges and Unique Stays

Elysian Retreat (Whitsundays)

An eco-luxury retreat situated on Long Island, offering a sustainable holiday experience amidst nature.

Sustainable Practice: Solar power, water conservation, and organic produce from the on-site garden. Guests can enjoy yoga sessions, spa treatments, and nature walks.

Spicers Hidden Vale (Grandchester)

An eco-friendly lodge set on a sprawling 12,000-acre property, blending luxury with a commitment to nature.

Enjoy delicious meals made from locally sourced ingredients. Engage in bushwalking, mountain biking, and farm experiences.

The Glasshouse (Montville)

A unique accommodation option offering stunning views of the Sunshine Coast and the Glass House Mountains. The lodge features floor-to-ceiling windows that blend indoor and outdoor living.
Guests can enjoy tailored experiences, including private dining and guided tours of the area.

Practical Tips for Choosing Accommodation

Consider proximity to attractions, public transport, and amenities when selecting where to stay.
Check reviews on trusted travel sites to gain insights into the quality of the accommodation and services offered.
Secure your accommodation in advance, especially during peak seasons or major events, to ensure availability and the best rates.

|16|

PLANNING YOUR TRIP

When planning a trip to Queensland, having a well-structured itinerary can help you maximise your experience. Whether you're visiting for a week or two, there are plenty of coastal highlights, islands, and outback adventures to enjoy. Here's a guide to creating a one-week and two-week itinerary, along with a packing checklist and budgeting tips.

Two-Week Itinerary

Day 1: Arrive in Brisbane

Explore the South Bank Parklands, visit the Queensland Art Gallery and Gallery of Modern Art (QAGOMA). Enjoy dinner at a riverside restaurant.

Day 2: Gold Coast

Head to the Gold Coast, spend the day at Surfers Paradise Beach. Visit a theme park like Warner Bros. Movie World or Sea World.

Day 3: Moreton Island

Take a day trip to Moreton Island. Activities include snorkelling, sandboarding, and visiting the Tangalooma Wrecks.

Day 4: Byron Bay

Drive to Byron Bay, explore the town, and hike to Cape Byron Lighthouse for stunning coastal views. Relax at one of the many beautiful beaches.

Day 5: Noosa

Travel to Noosa, spend time at Noosa National Park, and visit the famous Noosa Main Beach. Enjoy shopping and dining at Hastings Street.

Day 6: Fraser Island

Join a guided day tour to Fraser Island. Explore Lake McKenzie, Eli Creek, and the Maheno Shipwreck.

Day 7: Return to Brisbane

Visit the Lone Pine Koala Sanctuary or take a scenic river cruise.

Depart from Brisbane.

Day 8: Travel to Cairns

Fly from Brisbane to Cairns, explore the Esplanade Lagoon and local markets.

Day 9: Great Barrier Reef

Take a full-day tour to the Great Barrier Reef for snorkelling or diving.

Day 10: Daintree Rainforest

Join a guided tour to the Daintree Rainforest and Cape Tribulation. Explore walking trails and spot wildlife.

Day 11: Kuranda

Take the scenic Kuranda Skyrail or the Kuranda Scenic Railway. Visit the markets and wildlife parks.

Day 12: Atherton Tablelands

Explore the waterfalls and lush landscapes of the Atherton Tablelands, including Millaa Millaa Falls and Lake Eacham.

Day 13: Outback Queensland

Travel to Longreach, visit the Australian Stockman's Hall of Fame, and take a sunset cruise on the Thompson River.

Day 14: Charleville and Departure

Explore Charleville's attractions, such as the Cosmos Centre. Fly out from either Charleville or return to Brisbane for departure.

Packing Checklist

Clothing

Pack essentials: breathable tops and shorts for warm days, swimwear, beachy cover-ups and a light layer for chilly evenings.

- Comfortable walking shoes and sandals
- Sunhat and sunglasses

Toiletries

- Sunscreen and lip balm with SPF
- Insect repellent
- Personal hygiene products

Travel Essentials

- Passport and identification
- Travel insurance documents
- Phone and charger
- Camera for capturing memories
- Reusable water bottle

Miscellaneous

- Guidebook or maps
- Snacks for day trips
- Swimmers and snorkelling gear (if not renting)

Budgeting Tips

Transport

Use public transport or consider renting a car for flexibility. Book domestic flights in advance for the best rates.

Food and Dining

Enjoy meals at local eateries or cook your own meals if staying in hostels or lodges with kitchen facilities.

Travel Insurance

Invest in travel insurance to cover unexpected cancellations or medical expenses, ensuring peace of mind during your trip.

|16|

ESSENTIAL QUEENSLAND TRAVEL FAQS

When travelling to Queensland, it's important to be prepared and informed. Here are some essential FAQs covering currency, language, local etiquette, health tips, emergency contacts, and useful apps to enhance your travel experience.

Currency

The official currency in Queensland is the Australian Dollar. It is abbreviated as AUD and is divided into 100 cents. ATMs are widely available, and credit cards are accepted in most places, though it's advisable to carry some cash for small purchases.

Language

The primary language spoken in Queensland is English. However, due to its multicultural population, you may also hear a variety of other languages spoken in different communities.

Local Etiquette

A simple "hello" or "g'day" is common. A handshake is often used when meeting someone for the first time. Tipping is appreciated but not obligatory. A tip of 10-15% is customary in restaurants if you are happy with the service.

Queenslanders take pride in their natural environment, so it's important to respect wildlife and follow local guidelines in national parks and reserves.

Health and Travel Insurance Tips

Ensure routine vaccinations are up to date. Depending on your travel history, consult your doctor about specific vaccines.

The sun can be intense, so wear sunscreen, hats, and protective clothing to avoid sunburn.

Emergency Contacts

In case of an emergency, dial 000 for police, fire, or ambulance services.

Familiarise yourself with the nearest hospital or medical centre in the area where you'll be staying.

Made in the USA
Monee, IL
03 January 2025

76006393R00056